GUESS THE COVERED WORD
FOR THIRD GRADE

by
Joyce Kohfeldt
Helen S. Collier

Editors
Louise Vaughn
Joey Bland
Tracy Soles

Table of Contents

KEY

B = words found at the **beginning** of sentences

M = words found in the **middle** of sentences

E = words found at the **end** of sentences

* = lesson written in paragraph(s)

PLUS: a list of initial consonants, blends, and
digraphs for each covered word in the lesson

Introduction

Learning to read continues to be a great adventure in third grade. Emphasis begins to shift from just learning to read and toward reading to learn. Reading is required throughout the day in all subject areas. Students need to "read" and "comprehend" the data in a graph in math class. They need to select essential information from irrelevant data to do story problems. Reading becomes either an exciting, positive part of a student's life in school and at home, or it is more like a toothache that occurs with every assignment. Students experiencing difficulty would not think of reading during free time for pleasure. They see other students completing assignments much quicker, and as a result begin to question their own abilities.

Successful students this age enjoy reading alone, with a partner, in a small group like a literature circle, or with the whole class in a choral reading. Third graders still enjoy a teacher read-aloud.

Third graders' free-time reading choices include picture books geared for older students (like the *Magic School Bus* series), nonfiction selections, and novels on a full range of topics and by a variety of authors.

What does Guess the Covered Word have to offer this wide range of third grade students with varying interests and differing skill levels? Reading, like learning to swim, is a complex skill that requires a range of prerequisites, many instructional opportunities, a range of practice and integration time, and ongoing assessment and monitoring. Reading and swimming are both tasks that different individuals master at different ages, and to differing degrees of proficiency.

When mastering swimming you cannot sit beside the pool and practice breathing for a day, kick your feet on dry land on the weekend, and move your arms in the air. These necessary components to swimming cannot be mastered in isolation or in any place other than water. The novice swimmer, whatever the age might be, begins in shallow water and often uses water wings to help stay afloat.

After mastering the basics, the swimmer moves to deeper water and learns new strokes. Soon, swimming has become a great hobby or a skill that may even lead to a related occupation.

Reading too is a complex skill. You cannot practice phonics on worksheets some days, comprehension questions from a book on Tuesdays, and other isolated vocabulary development activities on still other days. **You cannot practice and apply the skills just during reading time. You must see how to transfer them to science, social studies, and math class.**

Guess the Covered Word offers students at any age, a cross-checking strategy that combines comprehension, context clues, and phonics. The examples, instruction, and practice of the Guess the Covered Word strategy appear in science, social studies, general themes, and math, as well as with literature connections.

Learning to read is a complex task that requires a variety of skills, experience and practice. Reading requires the following:

- comprehension, thinking, and processing meaning (Students must expect print to make sense and must perceive the reader's job to include rereading and self-correcting when the text, as it is being read, fails to make sense.)
- visual discrimination and the understanding of print concepts (speech bubbles; north, south, east, and west on a map; horizontal and vertical axes on a graph; or a cutaway diagram in science)
- visual and auditory skills of recognizing letter patterns and groupings like prefixes and suffixes, developing a visual sense for sounds that have more than one spelling pattern (hair and hare; there, their, and they're)
- knowing what to do when you bump into an unknown word while reading instead of randomly guessing
- utilizing both illustration and text to explore the full meaning of what is being read

Some third graders read along without difficulty when meeting words that are part of their sight vocabulary. When they bump into an unknown word, however, they may resort to one of the following:

- **They may stop in their tracks and look up at the teacher with a "rescue me" expression on their faces.** They stop being problem solvers and look to an "outside expert" for assistance. They either do not know (or choose not to use) any independent strategies. These readers are most at risk because they do not know how to proceed without an adult present.

- **They may try to sound out the word, letter by letter, and then blend the sounds back into a word.** In some cases this will work (c-a-t...cat). Many letter combinations, however, form sounds that are different from the sum of their individual letter sounds (c-h-a-r-t...ch-ar-t; s-t-a-t-i-o-n... st-a-tion). These readers use a "phonics only" approach that does not always work in English.

- **They may make a wild guess, substituting any word under the sun without expecting it to make sense.** This is not only a poor habit to form as a reader, but it also disrupts the flow of comprehension.

- **They may ask themselves, "What would make sense?" and substitute that word for the unknown word without looking carefully at the letters in the word or using phonics.** For these students, the flow of comprehension is left intact, but they do not develop the skills of decoding new words independently. When the new words they meet are in contexts of which they have little or no prior knowledge, this strategy will not work.

- **They may look at the word's beginning sound and say any word that starts with that sound.** They do not consider the other letters in the word or if the word makes sense in the context in which it was found. This strategy also leads to major disruption in the flow of comprehension since these "off the wall" substitutions seldom make sense.

The Guess the Covered Word strategy is a more systematic and comprehensive strategy than those just described. Guess the Covered Word is a cross-checking strategy that combines both context clues and word analysis skills to decode unknown words. It teaches the student to ask three basic questions when confronting new words:

1. **What makes sense?**

2. **How long is the word?**

3. **How does the word begin (up to the first vowel)? Are there any prefixes, suffixes, or known "little" words, and what are all the other letters in the word?**

If you have been using the Four-Blocks™ Literacy Model developed by Patricia M. Cunningham and Dorothy P. Hall, then Guess the Covered Word will not be new to you. The Four Blocks described in their balanced literacy model for grades 1-3 include Guided Reading, Self-Selected Reading, Writing, and Working with Words. The Working with Words block contains several strategies and activities that promote both reading and spelling; Guess the Covered Word is one of the reading strategies introduced. It is a cross-checking strategy that combines using sentence meaning (context clues), word length, and phonics to unlock new words. The strategy may be found in several publications, such as *The Teacher's Guide to the Four Blocks™* by Patricia M. Cunningham, Dorothy P. Hall, and Cheryl Sigmon; *Month-by-Month Phonics for Third Grade* by Patricia M. Cunningham and Dorothy P. Hall; *Word Wall "Plus" for Third Grade* by Patricia M. Cunningham, Dorothy P. Hall, and Joyce Kohfeldt; and *Phonics They Use* by Patricia M. Cunningham.

Regardless of whether or not you have been using the Four-Blocks™ Literacy Model, Guess the Covered Word will help your students know what to do when they are reading and bump into a word they do not know. **This resource was written to support any teacher working with students in** third grade, ESL students who are older, or elementary students with special needs who are reading at the early fluent level.

- The themes and topics were selected to be consistent with those taught in third grade classrooms across the country.

- The interest level of early fluent readers, eight and nine years old, influenced each lesson, including the chosen literature.

- The high-frequency words were taken from *Month-by-Month Phonics for Third Grade* by Patricia M. Cunningham and Dorothy P. Hall.

- The examples come from real classrooms and were field tested with real students.

- The lessons represent a wide range of challenges for third graders. Some examples are easier, using sentences with easier words at the end and in the middle as the covered words. These examples will support the learning of at-risk readers and those who are being introduced to the strategy for the first time in third grade. Other examples are more challenging, with previously unexplored topics, lessons written in paragraphs, and more of the covered words in the middle and beginning of the sentences.

- Examples of possible guesses made by students in third grade have been included in the appendix (pages 62-64). The range of these words, as well as the range of guesses you are likely to hear from your own students, will illustrate how Guess the Covered Word challenges the full range of learners in any third grade.

Teachers from across the country often voice their difficulty in finding time to do everything they need to do. In a balanced literacy program there is direct instruction in both reading and writing. Students also have opportunities to apply what they have learned as they read and write. The ability of students to unlock new words as they read, and spell new words as they write, plays an integral part in a balanced program. Guess the Covered Word is an essential cross-checking reading strategy that uses the best brain research, and includes both context clues and phonics.

This resource, *Guess the Covered Word for Third Grade*, provides examples to show how the strategy of Guess the Covered Word can be used throughout the day and applied in multiple content areas and settings.

GUESS THE COVERED WORD CAN BE USED IN THESE AREAS

- **Social Studies**, where students are reading and meeting new content words like "communities" and "Australia."

- **Science**, where lots of new words like "exploration" or "astronaut" pop up and challenge young readers.

- **Math**, where students are exposed to many words like "multiplicand" or "numerator" which are not part of their everyday listening or speaking vocabularies.

- **Themes** or units, where new words like "traditions" or "Kwanzaa" might surface.

- **Literature Links** within a shared reading, a read-along, or guided reading lesson.

GENERAL DIRECTIONS FOR TEACHING A GUESS THE COVERED WORD LESSON

Guess the Covered Word lessons have more than one level of difficulty based on the level of phonics knowledge needed, the placement of the covered word in the sentence, and whether sentences versus paragraphs are used for context. The easiest lessons are covered words that begin with a single consonant, while more advanced lessons contain covered words with blends or digraphs.

The easiest lessons also have the covered word located at the end of a sentence. More advanced lessons may have the covered word located in the middle of the sentence, while sentences with the covered word at the beginning are the most difficult. If the word is in the middle or near the beginning of a sentence, another step will be added to the procedure (see "Introducing the Strategy if the Covered Word is at the Beginning or Middle of the Sentence," page 7).

Easier lessons also use simple sentences, while more advanced lessons may include covered words within a paragraph. It is easier for students to use the Guess the Covered Word strategy with simple sentences than in a paragraph, where information or clues from earlier sentences may be useful or necessary to determine the covered word.

The Table of Contents contains information about the difficulty level of each lesson. You can select examples written as sentences or paragraphs, as well as examples with covered words in the beginning, middle, end, or all three.

By third grade, most students should be able to meet the challenge of words that begin with consonants, blends, and digraphs. If this is your students' first exposure to the strategy, consider starting with simple sentences where many of the covered words appear at the ends of sentences.

TEACHER PREPARATION

- Choose a Guess the Covered Word example from a ready-to-use transparency or copy a black-and-white example onto a sheet of transparency film.

Amelia is a nine-year-old girl who has just **transferred** to a new school in a new community.

- Use sticky notes or small pieces of paper (easily stored in a plastic bag for continuous use) to cover the bold words in the lesson. If the word to be covered begins with a consonant, digraph, or blend, use a separate sticky to cover those consonants (onset) that come before the first vowel.

Use another sticky note to cover the rest of the word (rime), beginning with the vowel. Cut or tear the sticky notes to be only as long as the word since word length is one of the strategy steps.

Amelia is a nine-year-old girl who has just ▢ ▢ to a new school in a new community.

INTRODUCING THE STRATEGY IF THE COVERED WORD IS AT THE END OF THE SENTENCE

- **Ask students to share with the class what they do when they are reading and bump into a word they do not know. Ask them to also share how well they think their "plans" work.** Record the responses, including each student's name and the suggested plan, on an overhead or chart paper. This is excellent diagnostic information that will help you tailor instruction to the specific needs of your class at this time. You may find that many say they just skip the word and go on. Others may say they try to sound it out and then go on. Some may look for smaller words in the new word and try to piece them together. Still others may just make wild guesses without using phonics at all. Notice that none of the "plans" just listed employs any second cross-check to see if the word makes sense.

- **Tell students that today's lesson will introduce a "strategy" with three steps that will help them when they bump into a word they do not know.** Explain that it is a very grown-up strategy that will require them to do more than one thing to determine what the word might be.

- **On the overhead projector, display the transparency with the covered word. Read the sentence to the class and put in an "mmm…" sound when you come to the "unknown word."**

- **Ask students to guess words that would make sense in the space covered in the sentence.** Record only those suggestions that make sense on the transparency near the covered word.

- **Have the class check word length by looking at the amount of space covered by sticky notes and comparing it to the visual length of the words they have guessed.** Cross out any words that are not the correct length. Add any other words that make sense and are the correct length. This step helps students who guess "dad" when the word is "father."

- **Remove the first sticky note and show the beginning letter(s), or onset.** Cross-check to see which of the guessed words makes sense, seems to be the correct length, and begins with the correct letter(s). Cross out the guessed words that do not begin with the uncovered beginning letter(s). If the covered word has not yet appeared as a guess, you may record additional guesses now that the onset is known.

- **Then, uncover all the letters to reveal the covered word.**

- **Reread the sentence and confirm that the word makes sense and matches the letters.** You will be pleased to hear students clap and cheer for themselves when they guess the covered word correctly. If students don't guess the word you might say, "The word is _____, and it means _____. That was a hard one!" Continue with the rest of the sentences, making sure that students understand the steps and the order to be used.

- **By the end of five or six sentences you should be able to ask, "What should we do next?" and students should be able to verbalize the strategy.** This is an important step in getting them to use the cross-checking strategy independently.

- Students need to be praised for using the three-step strategy. The focus of the lesson initially needs to be on the steps in the strategy, not on the individual words. **Students need to talk about how the three steps allowed them to figure out the word and keep comprehension going as they read.**

- Most students this age will require many teacher-directed, whole-class, or small-group practice sessions with the strategy for it to become part of their reading behavior at the automatic level.

> ### Extra Procedural Step:
>
> **If the "unknown word" is in the middle or near the beginning of a sentence, do this:**
>
> 1. Put your finger on the "unknown word" to keep your place.
> 2. Reread the beginning of the sentence and put in an "mmm" sound when you come to the unknown word.
> 3. Read on to the end of the sentence to find more clues.
> 4. After reading both the beginning and end of the sentence, follow the same Guess the Covered Word strategy steps. Ask:
>   - What makes sense?
>   - How long is the word?
>   - How does the word begin (up to the first vowel)? Are there any prefixes, suffixes, or known "little" words, and what are all the other letters in the word?

How to Use This Book

This resource includes the following:

★ **12 ready-to-use, full-color transparencies,** including a transparency to introduce the strategy (as shown on the poster). The remaining eleven transparencies are examples involving science, social studies, math, literature, or general themes.

> The transparency showing the three-step strategy makes a great introductory whole-class lesson. In addition, select another transparency that matches a theme or topic currently being studied to provide some practice.

You can use a water-based transparency marker to record student guesses right on the transparency and then erase and reuse the transparency. If a permanent transparency marker is used by mistake, spray some hair spray on a cloth or paper towel and gently rub it over the words to remove them.

★ **26 Guess the Covered Word lessons** (pages 20-61) in five different categories: science, math, social studies, literature, and general themes. These lessons are ready to be made into transparencies on any copier. If you wish, color may be added to the illustrations or border with transparency markers that are permanent or water-based. The five categories were selected to illustrate how this strategy may be used throughout the day in all content areas.

★ **An Observation Recording Chart** (page 15) to help keep track of which students are utilizing the three-step Guess the Covered Word strategy in both teacher-directed and independent-reading situations. Make copies of the chart so it can be used many times. Knowing which students are not using some or any of the steps, either in teacher-directed activities or in independent-reading situations, will help you focus instruction on the areas requiring further teaching and practice.

Observing students during a teacher-directed Guess the Covered Word lesson, independent reading, or a conference makes it easy to record mastery of the strategy.

> Use a simple code to record your observations. For example, write an "M" for meaning when the first step is being used effectively, "WL" for word length when the second step is being used, and an "SA" for structural analysis when prefixes, suffixes, known "little" words, and all the letters of the word are considered. Mark an "I" if the observation is being made when the student is working independently and "TD" if the observation is being made during a teacher-directed lesson.

Teachers who carefully observe students who have difficulty in the early stages of reading, regardless of their age, will find students looking to them with a "rescue me" look, guessing wildly when their guesses do not make sense, and looking at the beginning sound and substituting any words that begin with that sound. Each of these responses is an indication of which steps need focused attention. The following list may assist some teachers in this observation and instructional decision-making process:

1. **Ask yourself, "What would make sense in this sentence?"** The student who tries to sound out the word letter by letter, and then blend the sounds back into a word needs this step. Sometimes words are irregular and don't follow any of the phonetic rules.

2. **Check the length of the word. Is it a long word or a short word?** All students can use this cross-checking strategy when meeting new words. It helps most after the "making sense" step. If the word "father" makes sense in the sentence but the word is short, a word like "dad" might work better.

3. **Look at all the letters at the beginning of the word that come before the first vowel and check for prefixes, suffixes, and known "little" words. Use your finger to**

cover the rest of the word. Now check out all the rest of the letters in the word. If a student asks himself "what makes sense" and substitutes that word without looking carefully at the covered word, he needs to focus his attention on the phonics component of the cross-checking strategy. Students may find themselves in situations where their prior knowledge and experience do not help them with "what makes sense," so the phonics step will need to be the first strategy for decoding the word.

The student who only looks at the beginning letter in the word and substitutes any word that starts with that letter, without using context clues for "making sense," also needs this strategy. Checking out *all* the letters in a word keeps the student from guessing a wrong word that may be the same as the right word except for one letter. Examples of these tricky words are words like **bitter**, **batter, better**, and **butter**.

★ **The Guess the Covered Word bookmarks** (page 17) can be strategy prompts for students as they learn the strategy, take it to the automatic level, and apply it throughout the day. They are also helpful for at-risk students who need more time and practice. The bookmarks can travel with a student to each reading piece, keeping the strategy steps before his/her eyes for easy reinforcement. **Making the strategy function at the automatic level is important, so the bookmark should not be kept as a long-term prompt.**

Third Grade Guess the Covered Word offers three different examples of bookmark strategy prompts. Some students will benefit from the bookmark with the mini illustrations from the poster. This strong visual bookmark with the strategy in its simplest form will support visual learners.

A second bookmark provides an example of a sentence with a covered word taken through all the steps. This one will provide support for any student who does not follow all the steps consistently. The example provides the type of support students feel in a teacher-directed lesson.

The third bookmark shows all the steps without the example and only has a small visual.

★ **Two awards** (page 18) have been included to recognize student application of the strategy. The finish line award recognizes students who have mastered the strategy steps. The award showing the go-cart recognizes students who are using the strategy independently.

Copy the appropriate award and give it to students "caught using the strategy effectively." Everyone enjoys positive reinforcement and recognition, especially those who need to work for longer periods of time to master the strategy's application.

★ **A full-color poster** is included to display in the room to remind students of the steps in the strategy. One effective way to display this poster might be at a center called Language Arts Tools. The poster could be the backdrop for this center that could contain an actual tool box with a small dictionary, electronic speller, extra Guess the Covered Word bookmarks, mini copies of the poster, the notebook reference card, and any other language arts tools you are currently expecting students to use. Sending them to the tool center when they run into a problem will get students in the habit of checking the steps on their own. Alternately, the poster may be placed in a highly visible area in the room so students will see the visual reminder often.

★ **A mini copy of the poster** (page 19) can be duplicated and given to students for their notebooks. The notebook reminder promotes independent learning at both school and at home for students who are not using the strategy at the automatic level.

★ **A copy of the Third-Grade Word Wall word list** (page 16) has been included. These high-frequency words occur often in the Guess the Covered Word lessons. The list of words appearing in each lesson can be found in the appendix (pages 62-64). Word Wall activities are also an integral part of the Working with Words block in the Four-Blocks™ Literacy Model.

★ **Reading Go-Cart Quick Reference** (page 14) is another example of a support which may be duplicated and given to students for their notebooks. The page can be used as it is or cut in half and placed on both sides of a 5" x 8" card for student use at home or at school.

★ **A "Dear Family" Letter** (page 13) is a connection between school and home that keeps family informed. By third grade students should be taking the major responsibility for their learning.

"PLUS" FACTORS

Third grade curriculum demands require an increase in the mental development skills associated with classification, collecting, comparing, and organizing information. Many of the Guess the Covered Word lessons at this level have challenging words and compound and complex sentences.

Many of the extension activities for that reason include collecting data, making predictions, working in cooperative groups or with a partner. Choose to use those that best meet the current needs of your students in the time that is available.

★ **Conservation:** Students in third grade need to become involved in collecting, recording, and reporting scientific information. Getting a commitment to conserve the water wasted while cleaning teeth shows students their power to influence grown-ups for an important cause.

★ **Our Planet of Plants:** Invite students to do a mini-search on amazing facts about plants. Getting into non-fiction resources in the media center will help as new topics arise in both science and social studies. Knowing that there are trees that are 4,700 years old may just peak their curiosity.

★ **Reasons for Rainbows:** Use a prism and a flashlight to create a rainbow. Model writing directions for this experiment with the whole class so they experience listing the necessary materials. Then, have students record the directions in the simplest form.

★ **Animal Hall of Fame:** Which of nature's creatures holds a title for the biggest, smallest, heaviest, tallest, or most amazing animal? Ask students to make predictions ahead of time, research the answers, then compare their findings to the predictions they made.

★ **Allowance:** Predict the most common ways eight-year-olds spend their allowance. Survey your class and see how many students get an allowance, and how they spend it.

★ **Selective TV Watching:** Survey the class to find out their favorite sports teams. For each sport, look at the team that had the most votes and discuss why that team is so popular.

★ **Estimate and Measure:** Select six familiar items found in any classroom to measure. Choose some interesting nonstandard measuring devices, like paper clips, foam peanuts, or Unifix® cubes, and compare the results to those using a ruler, tape measure, or yard stick.

★ **Reading A Graph:** Have your students create a graph to show which restaurants they think have the best fast food. Then, use a Venn diagram to compare the results from your class to the results shown on the graph from another third-grade class.

★ **Yummy Pizza:** Have students survey their own grade level or the teachers in the school to find out 1) the favorite type of crust, and 2) the favorite topping(s).

★ **Savings Through Advertisements:** Have students do home research, such as finding out 1) where each of their families shop, 2) why that location is selected, and 3) what kind of savings opportunities the store offers.

★ **Sleepovers and Campouts:** Poll the class for the number of students who have had a sleepover. Collect, graph, and describe facts about what they ate, what they did, and how many hours of sleep they got.

★ **Writing A Paper:** Make a list of overworked words (like, said, etc.) from a rough draft of a class assignment. Brainstorm lots of words that are replacements (whispered, yelled, whimpered, shouted, answered, told, etc.). Have each student edit a rough draft by circling each of the overworked words and replacing it with a more colorful word.

★ **Friendships:** Encourage students to think about who makes a good friend by finishing one of these "thinking stems."

Friends have things in common like....

Friends enjoy....

Friends usually like....

Friends always....

Friends never....

Select some of the resulting responses to read aloud.

★ **Who's In Charge?** Brainstorm and record with your class some important decisions that adults make for them. Explore a plan to make one or more of these into joint decisions, between teachers and parents on one end and students on the other. Have the class monitor how well the plan works.

★ **Cooperative Learning:** The ability to work together in groups provides greater cooperation, mutual respect, and greater achievement. Choose some assignments where small group involvement would be appropriate and have each group monitor how well they 1) listen to each other, 2) share responsibility, and 3) achieve the goals.

★ **"Air Jordan":** Choose a person who is a good role model and collect data on him/her from the media center, the Internet, or a Student Almanac, and write a brief report.

★ **Map Reading:** Select a couple of maps that have all the map elements on them. Divide the class into two teams, with each team working with one of the maps. Each team sends a member to the map. The same question is given to both teams so each can demonstrate understanding of the term by pointing to the element on the map and telling what it does or means. Each correct answer earns five points. Continue playing until one team scores 20 points.

★ **Bordering Neighbors:** Have students work as partners with a map of their state, Canada, or Mexico. Have them take turns asking border or boundary questions and use the map as their reference.

★ **Lon Po Po:** Use *Lon Po Po*, the Chinese version of *Little Red Riding Hood*, as a read-aloud or have it be a literature group choice. Have students discuss who they believe is more clever—the three girls in *Lon Po Po* or Little Red Riding Hood. The students might also compare the two stories including the characters, the setting, and the plot.

★ **Princess Furball:** *Princess Furball* is a Cinderella tale with a twist. Before reading this version, have students brainstorm how the main character may solve the problem. Then, read the story and compare the class endings with the one created by the author.

★ **Amelia's Notebook:** Amelia drew a ketchup bottle from multiple points of view (from the top looking down, from the side, etc.). Have students choose some common object and "see" it from more than one vantage point.

★ **Alexander Who Used To Be Rich Last Sunday:** Invite students to chart the spending of their allowance for a week. Then, let them compare their spending habits with a classmate's.

CREATING YOUR OWN GUESS THE COVERED WORD LESSONS

Once you and your class have experienced the power and pleasure of using the Guess the Covered Word strategy, you will want to create some of your own lessons to fit the other content you are studying. The lessons can be used with the whole class or small groups. If students create some examples, they can be made ready by applying sticky notes and used as a student-directed lesson or independent center activity. Some students might like to create their own examples and challenge family members to figure out the covered word(s).

Step 1 Choose a topic for your Guess the Covered Word.

Example topic: map reading

Step 2 Make a list of words that are important to the topic.

north	south	east
west	cardinal	scale
distance	key	title

compass rose

Step 3 **Determine the difficulty level.** Covered words are easiest at the end of a sentence, harder in the middle, and hardest at the beginning. Covered words that begin with single consonant onsets are easier to guess than those that begin with blends or digraphs. Simple sentences are easier than using the strategy in a paragraph where information or clues from earlier sentences may be useful or necessary in determining the covered word.

The following example is a paragraph with covered words at the middle and beginning of sentences (mid-level difficulty).

Step 4 **Write sentences with words selected to cover.** Make sure you selected words that begin with a consonant, blend, or digraph. In order for the strategy to be cross-checking, each covered word should be one for which more than one word makes sense in the sentence.

Reading **directions** on maps is an important skill. There are many different **types** of maps, but a few common things are found on most maps.

Step 5 **Cover each of the selected words with (1) a sticky note to cover the beginning letter(s) up to the first vowel, and (2) another sticky note to cover the remaining portion of the word.** Remember to make sticky notes only as long as the word, since word length is one of the strategy steps.

Reading ▢▢ on maps is an important skill. There are many different ▢▢ of maps, but a few common things are found on most maps.

Step 6 Follow the three steps to make sure your examples work:

1. Ask what words make sense in the sentence.
2. Check the word length.
3. Check the beginning letter(s), prefixes/suffixes, known "little" words, and all the other letters in the word.

Step 7 Challenge your class to "guess the covered words" in your lessons. If the lesson is being led by a student, remind him or her to coach the other students with the strategy steps if they need help.

Family Letter

_____
Date

Dear Family,

    I am becoming a good reader with both easy text and more complex reading material from my science and social studies books. Did you know that one of my favorite authors is

_____? I also really enjoy reading _____

(Author's Name)   (Author, Type of Literature, or Title)

_____.

    The words I meet are getting longer and longer. I have learned a strategy that helps me figure out new words. I will be bringing home a copy of the poster we use in class and a bookmark that reminds me to use the strategy whenever I read.

The strategy has three steps:

1. I cover the word with my finger or a sticky note and ask myself what words would make sense. I write down some of my guesses.

2. I look to see if the word is long or short. Then I check my list for words that are the right size.

3. I uncover and check the beginning letters up to the first vowel (a, e, i, o, u). I look to see if one of my guesses begins with those letters. I also check for prefixes, suffixes, and known "little" words. I then check all the letters in the word.

You can help me become a better reader by reading to me, and by listening to me read to you.

Love,

_____

Reading Go-Cart Quick Reference

Cut this sheet in half. Paste one half on the front of a 5-inch by 8-inch card. Paste the other half on the back of the card. This is your Quick Reference Card. You will find it is a handy tool to keep your reading go-cart rolling!

Guess the Covered Word

1. **Cover** the word that is stopping your cart.

2. Think about **what makes sense** in the sentence, in place of the word that you have covered.

3. Check the **length** of the word. How long or short should the covered word be to fit?

4. Check the **letter(s) at the beginning** of the word. Look for prefixes, suffixes, and known "little" words. Then, look at **all the other letters in the word**.

Guess the Covered Word

1. **Cover**

2. **What makes sense?**

3. **How long?**

4. **Letters and sounds**

Observation Chart

Code Key

M = Makes sense   **I** = Independent
WL = Checks word length   **TD** = Teacher Directed
SA = Structural Analysis (first letter(s), prefixes,
     suffixes, known "little" words, all the other letters
     in the word)
✓ = Uses all three steps in order consistently

Name	Date / Code		Date / Code		Comments
Jake	9/9	TD ✓	10/15	I ✓	Sentences automatic
Michael	9/9	TD SA	10/15	TD ✓	OK Check again
Juliana	9/9	TD M	10/15	TD M WL	Focus on what makes sense

Name	Date / Code	Date / Code	Date / Code	Comments

Word Wall Word List

(from *Month-by-Month Phonics for Third Grade* by Patricia M. Cunningham & Dorothy P. Hall, 1997)

about	hole	there
again	hopeless	they
almost	I'm	they're
also	impossible	thought
always	independent	threw
another	into	through
anyone	it's	to
are	its	too
beautiful	journal	trouble
because	knew	two
before	know	unhappiness
buy	laughed	until
by	let's	usually
can't	lovable	vacation
city	myself	very
could	new	want
community	no	was
confusion	off	wear
countries	one	weather
didn't	our	went
discover	people	were
doesn't	prettier	we're
don't	prettiest	what
enough	pretty	when
especially	probably	where
everybody	question	whether
everything	really	who
except	recycle	whole
exciting	right	winner
favorite	said	with
first	schools	won
friendly	something	won't
general	sometimes	wouldn't
getting	terrible	write
governor	that's	your
have	their	you're
hidden	then	

Bookmarks

FOLLOW THE STEPS TO GUESS THE COVERED WORD

Amelia is a nine-year-old girl who has just **transferred** to a new school in a new community.

Where is the word?
Cover the word to keep your place.

Amelia is a nine-year-old girl who has just ▓▓▓▓ to a new school in a new community.

What makes sense?
> moved
> come
> transferred

How long is the word?
Amelia is a nine-year-old girl who has just tr▓▓▓ to a new school in a new community.

How does the word begin? Are there any prefixes, suffixes, or known "little" words? What are the other letters in the word? Check your list.
> transferred

Did you guess the covered word?
> yes

© Carson-Dellosa

FOLLOW THE STEPS TO GUESS THE COVERED WORD

STOP
Where is the word? Cover the word to keep your place.

THINK
What makes sense?

LOOK
How long is the word?

LISTEN
How does the word begin? Are there prefixes, suffixes, or known "little" words? What are the other letters in the word? Check your list.
Did you guess the covered word?

© Carson-Dellosa

What do you do when you meet a reading roadblock? Follow the steps to guess the covered word!

STOP
Where is the word?
Cover the word to keep your place.

THINK
What makes sense?

LOOK
How long is the word?

LISTEN
How does the word begin?
Are there prefixes, suffixes, or known "little" words? What are the other letters in the word?

Check your list. Did you guess the covered word?

© Carson-Dellosa

Awards

Congratulations on crossing the finish line!

_____ is using the

Guess the Covered Word Strategy!

_____
(Signed)

_____
(Date)

© Carson-Dellosa

_____

is using the
Guess the Covered Word Strategy
as a reading tool in many reading tasks!

_____
(Signed)

_____
(Date)

© Carson-Dellosa

What do you do when you run into a word you don't know? Use the Guess the Covered Word steps to get

READY...SET...GO!

READY?

Where is the word?
Cover the word to keep your place.

My go-cart needs new ☐.

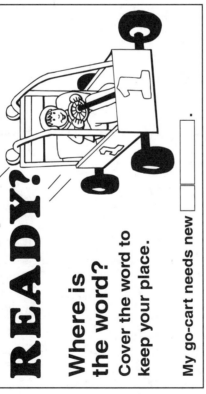

GO!

How long is the word?

My go-cart needs new ☐.

fenders   ~~paint~~   wheels   ~~tires~~

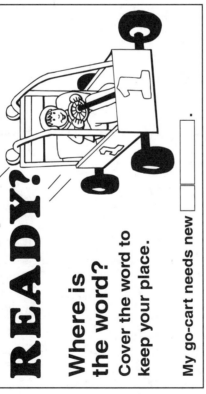

SET...

What makes sense?

My go-cart needs new ☐.

fenders   paint   wheels   tires

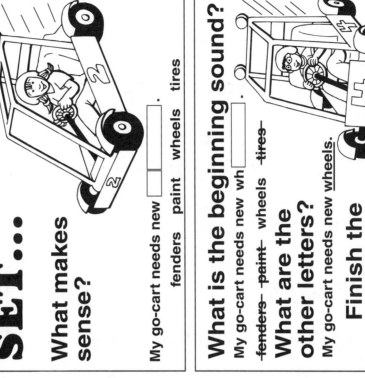

What is the beginning sound?
My go-cart needs new wh☐.

~~fenders~~   ~~paint~~   wheels   ~~tires~~

What are the other letters?
My go-cart needs new ☐.

My go-cart needs new <u>wheels</u>.

Finish the reading race!

Conservation

Do you ever wonder if third graders can make a difference in their **community?**

Think about being a **conservationist** who wants to conserve the earth's water. Start with something we all do **daily,** like brushing our teeth. **Predict** how much water is wasted if we allow the water to continuously run while we brush our teeth. Record your predictions, and then place a **container** in the sink to catch and measure the wasted water. Was your **prediction** close to the amount of water wasted?

20

Conservation (continued)

Multiply the amount of water **measured** by the number of times you brush your teeth in a week. Then, **figure** the amount of water wasted in a year. Take your **data** and total the same numbers for each person in your family. You may **discover** that the amount of wasted water is enormous.

Using a calculator, find the amount of water **wasted** by your third grade class each day as they brush their teeth. Wow! Third graders can make a difference just by **conserving** water while brushing their teeth.

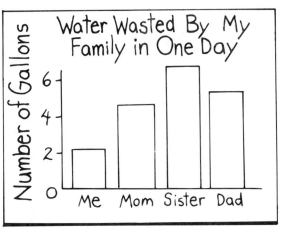

Spaced Out

Have your friends ever accused you of being "spaced out" and **teased** you with these questions: "What planet are you on? What solar system are you in?" Third graders are learning factual information and **serious** things about space and our solar system.

Our planet, Earth, and eight other known planets move in **paths** called orbits around a star that we know as the Sun. Our solar system **contains** nine planets and the Sun. Moons **travel** in orbits around the planets.

Sometimes third graders make **charts** or models of our solar system to help them learn how the planets compare in size and distance from the Sun.

22

Our Planet of Plants

Long ago, before there were any people on our planet, plants **grew** here. If you could look back as far as three billion years, you could see algae **growing** in or near the water. The first land **plants** appeared around 300 or 400 million years ago.

Plants grow in many **varieties** and are used for many different purposes. What are some things that we can say are **true** about all plants? Plants use air, **sunlight,** and water to make their own food. Most are **held** to their spots by roots. Cellulose keeps plants standing **straight.**

The oldest plants living today are the Bristlecone Pine trees which are 4,700 years old and found in **California.**

23

Enough Energy?

Has the power ever been off at your **house**? What a **problem** that can be! Think what it would be like if the power were off **worldwide**!

We need power for almost everything, and we don't even **think** about it until it isn't there.

Some scientists are very **concerned** that the Earth could run out of the fuel we need to make the power we depend on for survival.

They are looking for **sources** of energy that are renewable or cannot be used up.

List some fuel sources that can be **reused** or seem limitless like solar power.

24

Animal Hall of Fame

If there were an Animal Hall of Fame, you would find the 110-foot blue whale **claiming** the title of the World's Largest Animal. Its 209 tons make quite a **splash**!

Nearby, you might see the 13-foot-tall African elephant **proudly** tipping the scales at eight tons.

Across from the elephant, bumping its head on the **skylight,** the 19-foot-tall giraffe would look down at you.

Looking a little **grouchy,** the 345-pound ostrich might dare you to pick an argument. It expects you to know it is the largest bird as it **stretches** its nine-foot neck all the way up to look down its beak at you.

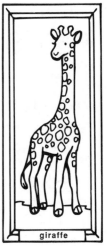

giraffe

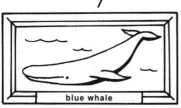

blue whale

ostrich

elephant

25

Allowance

Once a week, on **Saturday**, Annie receives her weekly allowance for completing chores like cleaning. So far this year, she has managed to save **twenty-four** dollars.

Annie might **spend** this week's $2.00 on a movie, as she has in the past. She could **deposit** it in her savings account where it earns interest. Annie's older sister has been **pestering** her about paying back the money she borrowed for Mom's gift. Annie still owes $5.00 and this might be the best time to **settle** the debt.

She is thinking carefully about her choices and **wonders** what advice you might give.

Selective TV Watching

The choices for what to watch when we turn on the television are **plentiful.** Some third graders enjoy **comedy** shows. Cartoons are also favorites because the cartoon **characters** show up in many places and are fun to collect. Exciting sports events have lots of **followers,** young and old. Basketball, **racing,** hockey, and gymnastics are a few favorites.

Survey your class to find out the favorite television shows.

Estimate and Measure

A contest challenged third graders to **predict** the answers to a variety of questions. Everyone was excited because both standard and unusual measurement **tools** would be used. Students worked **cooperatively** and estimated their answers. Then, they checked their predictions by using a measuring **device**.

The first **challenge** was to measure a pencil with a paper clip. Students argued that the challenge did not **state** the size of the paper clip. The class learned that a challenge needs to be written **precisely**.

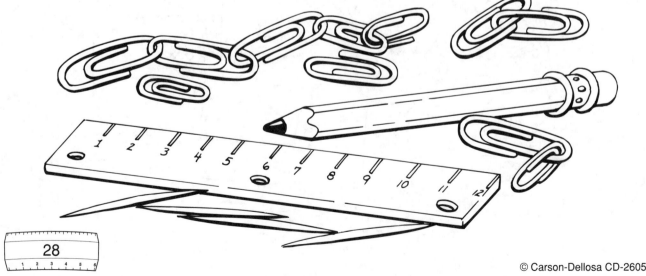

Estimate and Measure (continued)

Most of us have **problems** when we use unusual measurements. We are not used to measuring the **width** of a desk in toothpicks or the height of a soda can with our fingers.

See if your class finds it difficult to estimate a large measurement, like the **perimeter** of the classroom, using the foot size of a student and a teacher.

Decades, Centuries, and Millenniums

It was Sue's big sister Alice's **birthday.** Sue overheard her mother **teasing** her sister about getting older: "Just think, you will be two decades old in the first year of the new **millennium**!" Sue didn't pay much attention at the **moment.**

At school, Sue was in the math center doing a **challenging** puzzle where she had to match math vocabulary to numbers. She **chose** "century" and matched it with 100 years. She had heard on TV about "the new millennium," so she was **certain** that was 1,000 years.

She was unsure about "decade" until she remembered her mother's **discussion** with Alice. Since she **knew** Alice would be 20 on her birthday, a decade must be 10 years.

Reading a Graph

Twenty third graders were asked which **restaurant** had the best fast food. Their answers were put on a graph.

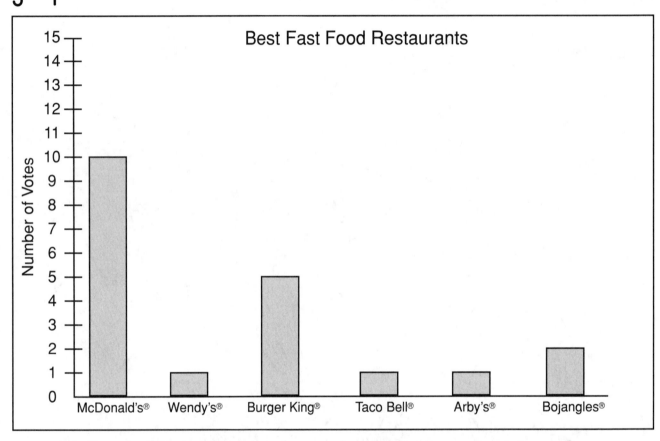

- Which fast-food **chain** has the most votes from third graders? _____

- Which restaurant **received** one-fourth of the total votes recorded? _____

Reading A Graph (continued)

- Which **place** accumulated one-half of the total votes? _____

- A **solitary** vote was received by each of which restaurants? _____

_____

   Predict what the results would be if the same question was asked of 20 third graders you know. **Collect** the data and record the results.

Example Graph   My Survey

   Compare the results of third graders in the example graph and the third graders you survey. Use a **Venn** diagram as the recording format.

Which restaurant has the best fast food?

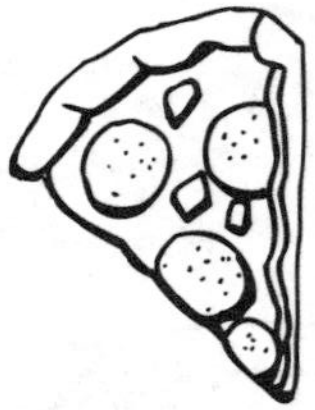

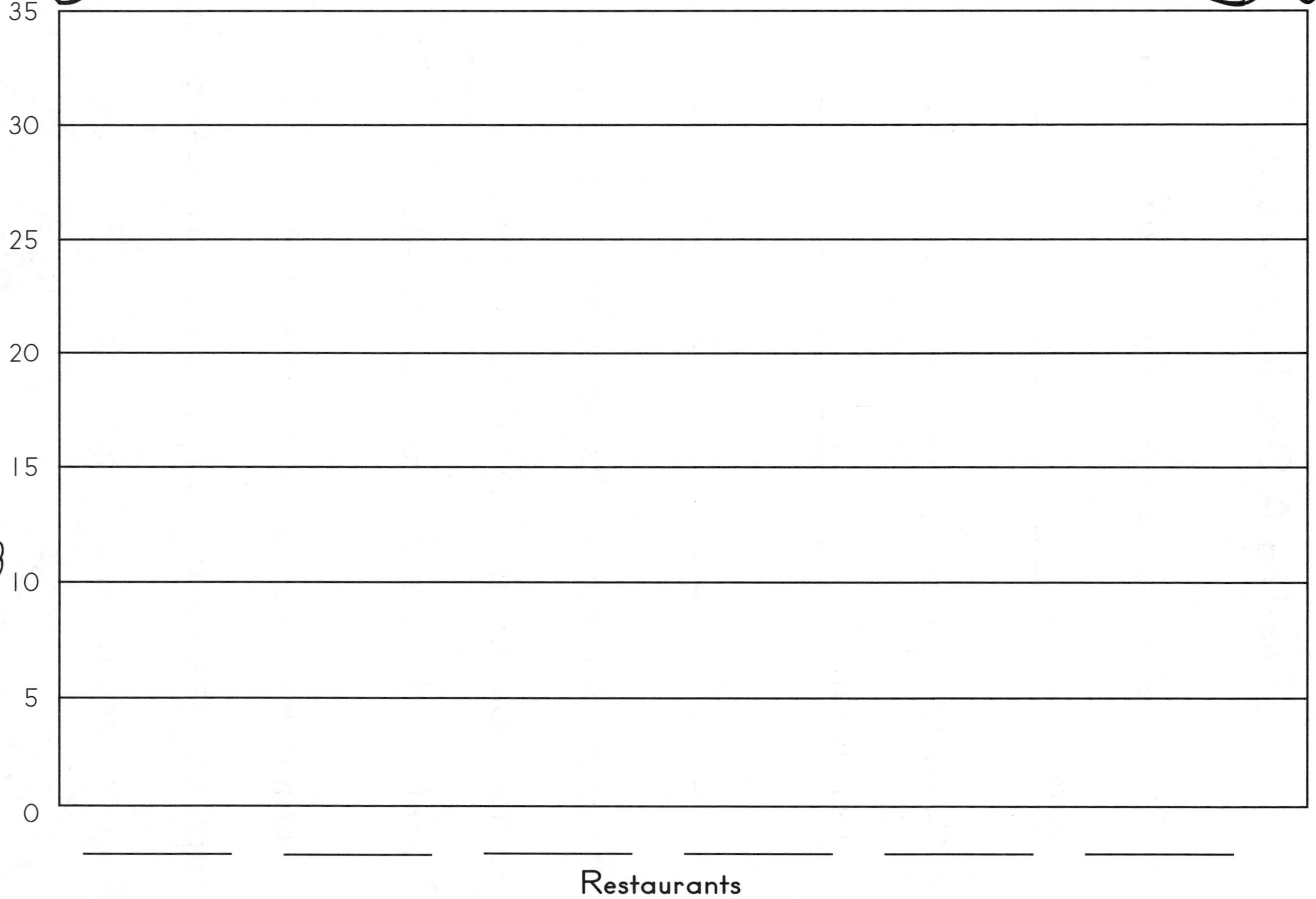

Number of Votes

35

30

25

20

15

10

5

0

Restaurants

34

Friendships

Each of us is very **fortunate** if we have some very special individuals to call friends. Friends are interested in similar activities like computers or **scouting.** They are there for each other **whether** they are winning or losing. They provide **comfort** when the going gets rough. Good friends are willing to share their time and **possessions.** They adopt newcomers and make them feel **welcome** in their group. Long-distance friendships are possible since **technology** makes it easier to stay in touch.

35

Friendships (continued)

Some friendships originate in **preschool** and last for a lifetime. **Classrooms** can provide the special place where students come into contact with people from many cultures and backgrounds different from their own. Learning to **respect** the uniqueness of individuals and their cultures provides opportunities for making new friends.

Individuals who are **challenged** in special ways need best friends and will be best friends. Blind friends help us "see" in new ways, while physically challenged friends show us the **fantastic** flexibility of the human body and soul.

36

Who's in Charge?

As third graders, sometimes we feel that the world is always advising or **telling** us what to do, how to do it, and when to do it. **Parents**, teachers, and other adults make many decisions for us. Sometimes we would just like the **freedom** to decide what to wear, what to do, what to say, and what to think. We would like to change some of those adult decisions into discussions that lead to **joint** decisions. What will it take to **begin** this shared responsibility?

A starting place might be to show adults that we can be responsible and honor the **promises** we make.

37

Who's in Charge? (continued)

Joint decisions on **rules** like bedtime, what we watch on television, when we do our homework, or who we visit are places to begin.

We would like more chances to make up our own minds about things that are **significant** to us. Selecting our clothing, choosing healthy foods, and using class time wisely are **personal** choices that we need to practice doing now as third graders.

Cooperative Learning

Learning together in small groups is fun and **productive.** The success of the group depends upon each person doing his or her **job.**

In a group, different people are assigned the jobs of reader, note taker, encourager, and **spokesperson.** The encourager makes sure that each **student** gets a chance to be heard. The timer helps the group use time wisely and keeps everyone on **schedule.** The note taker records all **responses** so everyone gets to contribute their ideas.

39

Cooperative Learning (continued)

The reader's job is to make sure that everyone **comprehends** the information being presented. The spokesperson **communicates** the thoughts of the group to the whole class.

In cooperative learning groups, **leadership** jobs are held by different people. Everyone has a **significant** part to play in the success of the group.

Map Reading

Why is it important to be **skilled** at map reading? There are as many reasons as there are **types** of maps. Maps can help you find your way to **specific** places and suggest interesting locations to visit. The distance scale helps you measure distances between places so you can estimate the time it will take from **departure** to arrival.

City maps show locations of **boulevards** and streets, important buildings, parks, train stations, and more. Landform maps show the positions of **mountains,** rivers, and lakes. Population and **product** maps are visual ways to illustrate specific facts and details.

Although there are many different **varieties** of maps, most of them have the same parts:

- Title: The title **states** what the map is about.

- Map key: The key shows the **symbols** and what they mean.

- Distance scale: This **scale** tells you how the distance between places compares to space on the map (for example, 1 inch = 50 miles).

- Compass rose: The compass rose shows the four **cardinal** directions – north, south, east, and west.

If you know how to interpret these map parts, you can **comprehend** almost any map you see.

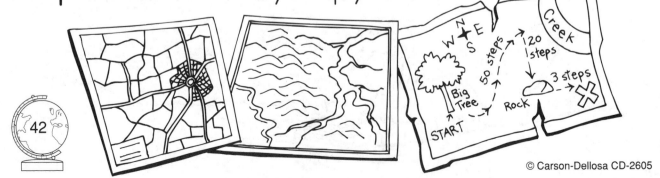

A Community of Responsible Citizens

People who live or work near each other need to **cooperate** and learn how to form a safe, peaceful community.

You may be a member of **several** communities at the same time like your classroom, your school, and your neighborhood communities.

The people in a community are its **citizens**.

The **government** of a community is a group of citizens who come together to make the community's rules or laws. Every member of a community has a responsibility to follow the **rules** of its government. Do you **follow** the rules?

Bordering Neighbors

Borders on a map show where one area or region ends and another begins. Usually, borders **separate** counties, states, provinces, or countries.

Boundaries, or borders, can be as **vast** as the Pacific Ocean, which is more than 64,000,000 square miles of water. A boundary can also be as small as a **checkpoint** into Canada, or a fence separating the United States and Mexico.

Canada, the United States, and Mexico all **share** the Pacific Ocean as their west-coast boundary. In Canada, the Hudson Bay forms a natural border for provinces like **Quebec** and Manitoba.

44

Bordering Neighbors (continued)

Some **locations** can be bordered by water or land or both. Colorado is bordered by seven states, including **Wyoming** and Kansas. Michigan is bordered by Indiana and several Great Lakes, including Lake **Superior.** In Canada, Quebec is bordered by the Hudson Bay and the Atlantic Ocean, as well as the province of **Newfoundland.** To the south of the United States, the Yucatan Peninsula has a land **boundary** with Mexico and a water border with the Gulf of Mexico.

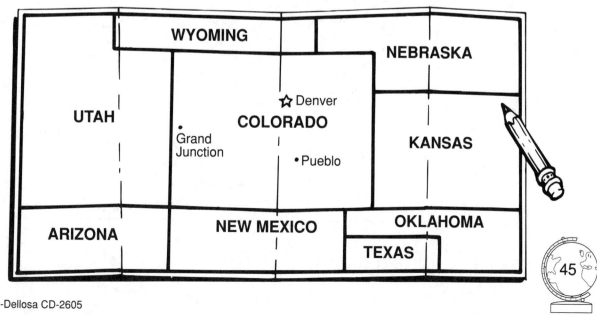

Bordering Neighbors Map

RUSSIA

Arctic Ocean

ICELAND

GREENLAND

Bering Sea

Baffin Bay

AK

Davis Strait

Yukon Territory

Northwest Territories

Labrador Sea

CANADA

Hudson Bay

Newfoundland

British Columbia

Alberta

Saskatchewan

Manitoba

Ontario

Quebec

Great Lakes

Pacific Ocean

WA

MT

ND

MN

ME

NH

VT

OR

ID

SD

WI

MI

NY

MA

RI

CT

PA

NJ

MD

NV

UT

WY

NE

IA

IL

IN

OH

WV

VA

CA

CO

KS

MO

KY

Atlantic Ocean

AZ

NM

OK

AR

TN

NC

SC

UNITED STATES

MS

AL

GA

TX

LA

FL

Gulf of Mexico

CUBA

HI

MEXICO

JAMAICA

Princess Furball

Princess Furball by Charlotte Huck (Turtleback Books, 1994)

Once upon a time, there was a **cruel** king whose wife had died and left him a baby daughter. He **chose** not to pay attention to his daughter because she reminded him of her mother. So the king ignored his daughter, who was sad and **lonely**. Her old nurse, who loved and cared for her, tried to make sure the little **princess** learned the things she should know. She grew up to be **beautiful** and very smart.

One sad day, the old nurse died and the king **promised** the princess to an ogre in exchange for fifty wagonloads of silver. The **furious** princess had a problem to solve.

Amelia's Notebook

Amelia's Notebook by Marissa Moss (Pleasant Company Publications, 1994)

Amelia was a nine-year-old girl who had just moved to a new home and **transferred** to a new school. Her mom gave her a **notebook,** thinking it would help Amelia feel better if she wrote about what she was thinking.

Amelia did not agree, but she **claimed** the notebook and started to write about how difficult it was to move. She put all **types** of illustrations in her notebook.

She did not share the **contents** from her notebook with anyone. It was **private.** Amelia's notebook was filled with trivia, feelings, and reflections such as you would write if you were keeping a **journal.** She wrote and drew pictures about her experiences and **travels.**

Amelia's Notebook (continued)

She **pasted** pictures, letters, postcards, and maps in her book. As other people saw what she was doing, they became very interested in her **fascinating** notebook. Some of her **peers** decided they wanted to keep journals, too.

Alexander Who Used to Be Rich Last Sunday

Alexander Who Used to Be Rich Last Sunday by Judith Viorst (Aladdin Books, 1980)

On Sunday, Alexander and his two brothers each received a dollar from visiting **relatives.** His parents **suggested** he save the money for something special. He realized that saving the money would be difficult after he thoughtlessly **wasted** money on bubble gum. Fifteen cents had **vanished** from his dollar.

Alexander made silly **predictions** with his family about things like how long he could hold his breath. Renting a pet snake from a **neighbor** was not too bright, either. His money was **disappearing** rapidly!

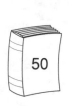

50

Alexander Who Used to Be Rich Last Sunday
(continued)

When he learned that his siblings still had their money, Alexander was **furious.** His father heard him **shouting** some ugly things and fined him the rest of his money. Alexander was once again **penniless** and very frustrated.

Sootface

Sootface: An Ojibwa Cinderella Story by Robert D. San Souci (Bantam Doubleday Dell Books for Young Readers, 1994)

Sootface was the youngest **daughter** in her Native American family. Her two older sisters were **cruel** and lazy. They made Sootface do most of the **chores** and they pushed her face into the ashes from the fire. She was **frightened** and wanted to get away.

A mighty warrior lived with his sister across the lake from the **village** where Sootface lived. He had been given the **power** to become invisible. The news spread that he was looking for a **wife**. He would marry the woman who could describe him because this would **prove** that she was honest.

Sootface (continued)

The two older sisters and other young women from the village each tried to look **beautiful** as they headed off to visit with the invisible warrior. All were **dishonest** when they said they could see the invisible warrior.

Without anything special to wear, Sootface went to **locate** the warrior. She was at the lake when she **noticed** the warrior's sister. As they were talking, Sootface saw a **handsome** man walking toward them. She **correctly** described the man who was the invisible warrior, so they were married and lived happily ever after.

Third Graders

Third graders are **somewhere** in the middle at the elementary school, not the youngest or the oldest. They are old enough to make independent choices about their friends, clothes, and food **preferences.** Being fair is an important part of their dealings with grown-ups.

Many eight- and nine-year-olds have best friends with whom they spend lots of time, enjoying sports, music, or **gymnastics.** These best friends like to spend time at each other's houses and on the **phone.**

Some third graders are regular **chatterboxes.** They love to talk about a wide range of **topics.**

54

Third Graders (continued)

Third graders are both competitive and **collaborative.** They like teamwork when they work together to complete **projects.** Some students serve as readers or **recorders** in cooperative groups, while others contribute their artistic abilities.

Although they can read , third graders still enjoy having the teacher do "read-alouds" by their **favorite** authors. They also enjoy reading to younger **siblings.**

Sleepovers and Campouts

Have you ever wanted to have a sleepover or campout at your house?

Convincing parents to give their permission may take some negotiating.

Selecting those to be invited is the next decision to be made.

Choosing lots of videos and computer games makes for good entertainment.

Snacks and treats make a sleepover or campout a success because everybody enjoys munching.

Popcorn disappears like magic, almost instantaneously.

56

Sleepovers and Campouts (continued)

Promises to go to sleep by midnight are forgotten as games, stories, and video watching seem to go on endlessly through the night.

Silence takes over as exhaustion finally wins and individuals drop off to sleep.

Daylight finds many yawning individuals eating cereal and waffles.

The **conclusion** is unanimous. Sleepovers and campouts are awesome!

Writing a Paper

It's a **challenge** to write a good paper.

Selecting a good topic sometimes causes difficulty.

Narrowing the topic is an important early step.

Taking notes, staying organized, and writing a rough draft take time.

Circling words you are not sure how to spell helps when you proofread.

Proofreading for capitalization, punctuation, and spelling is easier with a computer.

Replacing overworked vocabulary with more interesting words makes a paper sound better.

Several main ideas and lots of details make a report complete.

58

Similes

Karen is as **strong** as a majestic lion.

Tex can **flip** like a dolphin when he is happy.

Jennifer likes to race like a fast **cheetah**.

Carmen is as **beautiful** as a colorful peacock.

When Jose is scared he **trembles** like a rabbit.

Doris is **clever** like a sly fox.

Rachel is **smart** like a wise owl.

Annie is funny like a **clown**.

59

Memories

Some memories are **treasures** we keep forever. If we don't make careful plans to **capture** them, memories can slip away and be lost. Carefully **preserved** memories can become more meaningful as time passes and we enjoy them over and over.

Some ways we can save memories are **through** picture albums, letters, scrapbooks, videos, diaries, or journals. Any kind of records we make, or things we **draw** or write down, are there to read and view again and again.

Memory Treasures

When Jennifer was about eight, she formed a **club** with four of her friends called "The Five-Girls Club." Years later, when Jennifer was all grown up, her mother found the club's record book **tucked** away in its hiding place under the stairs. She **wrapped** it as a Christmas gift and gave it to Jennifer. One of the other members of the club was **present** when it was opened.

Jennifer and her friend read the book aloud, laughed, and remembered as they revisited the days of their **childhood**. The **journal** told of keeping minutes, excluding boys from membership, and voting on the club's rules. The journal was a **special** memory treasure for everyone.

Appendix

Pages 20-21—Conservation

community .... neighborhood, city, town
conservationist ... scientist, person
daily .... often, frequently
predict .... guess, estimate
container .... cup, glass, bowl
prediction .... guess, estimate
measured .... estimated, collected
figure .... add, calculate
data .... information, observations
discover .... find, learn
wasted .... lost
conserving .... saving
• High-frequency words: their, about, by, to, with, something, our, was, community, who, want(s), your, then

Page 22—Spaced Out

teased .... bugged, bothered
serious .... important, true
paths .... routes, trails, tracks
contains .... includes, has
travel .... move, revolve
charts .... illustrations, pictures
• High-frequency words: have, your, with, are, questions, what, our, sometimes, about, know

Page 23—Our Planet of Plants

grew .... lived, survived
growing .... forming, sprouting
plants .... vegetation, sprouts
varieties .... mixtures, types
true .... real, facts
sunlight .... light, sunshine
held .... fastened, tied, kept
straight .... up, tall
California .... North Carolina, Texas
• High-frequency words: before, there, our, were, could, first, are, their, by, people, what, about

Page 24—Enough Energy?

house .... home, school, office
problem .... pain, mess
worldwide .... everywhere
think .... worry, wonder
concerned .... worried, sure
sources .... kinds, varieties
reused .... recycled, reclaimed
• High-frequency words: your, what, were, off, almost, everything, about, until, there, are, very, could, they, don't

Page 25—Animal Hall of Fame

claiming .... holding
splash .... sight, picture
proudly .... happily, uniquely
skylight .... ceiling, roof
grouchy .... mean, unhappy
stretches .... extends, pushes
• High-frequency words: there, were, to, know, its

Page 26—Allowance

Saturday .... Monday, Friday
twenty-four ..... eighteen, ten
spend .... use, blow
deposit .... put
pestering .... bugging, asking
settle .... pay, repay
wonders .... asks
• High-frequency words: could, where, about, what

Page 27—Selective TV Watching

plentiful .... many, numerous
comedy .... funny, mystery
characters .... animals, people
followers .... fans
racing .... footfall, skating
survey .... check, ask
• High-frequency words: what, when, are, also, favorite(s), because, have, to, your

Pages 28-29—Estimate and Measure

predict .... guess, estimate
tools .... devices
cooperatively .... individually, together
device .... tool
challenge .... problem
state .... say, tell
precisely .... carefully, exactly
problems .... difficulty, trouble
width .... length, perimeter
perimeter .... width, length
• High-frequency words: to, question(s), was, because, their, then, by, first, with, when, are, our, your

Pages 30-31—Decades, Centuries, and Millenniums

birthday .... graduation, anniversary
teasing .... bugging, kidding
millennium ...... year, decade
moment .... time
challenging ...... hard, difficult, fun
chose .... picked, selected
certain .... positive, sure
discussion .... talk
knew .... understood
• High-frequency words: was, about, getting, two, first, new, didn't, school, where, to, with, about, until, knew

Pages 32-33—Reading a Graph

restaurant .... place, stop
graph .... chart
chain .... place, restaurant
received .... got, has
place .... restaurant, stop
solitary .... single
predict .... guess, estimate, tell
collect .... get, gather
compare .... check
Venn .... circle, bar
• High-frequency words: were, their, was, what, question, know, by

Pages 35-36—Friendships

fortunate .... lucky, special
scouting .... baseball, skating, gymnastics
whether .... if
comfort .... support, help
possessions .... stuff, junk, toys, things
welcome .... wanted, good, special
technology ...... Internet, phones, faxes, computers
preschool .... nursery, kindergarten, childhood
classrooms .... school, scouting
respect .... appreciate, treasure, enjoy
challenged .... unique, handicapped
fantastic .... amazing, incredible
• High-frequency words: very, have, to, are, they, there, whether, when, their, where, with, new, who, into

Pages 37-38—Who's in Charge?

telling .... advising, ordering
parents .... mothers, fathers, uncles
freedom .... chance, opportunity
joint .... shared
begin .... start
promises .... deals, agreements
rules .... limits
significant .... important, relevant
personal .... individual
• High-frequency words: sometimes, always, what, when, wear, into, to, our, who, are, about

Pages 39-40—Cooperative Learning

productive .... useful, enjoyable
job .... part, responsibility
spokesperson .... timer, leader
student .... person, boy, girl
schedule .... task, time, track
responses .... answers, ideas
comprehends .... understands, hears
communicates .. tells, shares, passes
leadership .... important, necessary
significant .... important, necessary, big
• High-frequency words: people, to, thought(s), whole, are, by, their

Pages 41-42—Map Reading

skilled .... good, efficient
types .... kinds, styles, examples
specific .... special, unique
departure .... starting, beginning
boulevards .... streets, malls
mountains .... hills, beaches
product .... state, road, continent
varieties .... kinds, types, styles
states .... says, tells
symbols .... pictures, illustrations
scale .... chart, line
cardinal .... main, basic
comprehend ..... understand, read
• High-frequency words: to, there, are, your, what,
about, know, these, almost

Page 43—A Community of Responsible Citizens

cooperate .... share
several .... many, other
citizens .... members
government ...... leadership
rules .... laws
follow .... obey
• High-frequency words: people, who, to, community,
are, your, school, its

Pages 44-45—Bordering Neighbors

borders .... boundaries, lines
separate .... divide, define, show
vast .... large, wide
checkpoint .... checkpoint
share .... have, claim
Quebec .... Newfoundland, Alberta
locations .... places, cities, countries
Wyoming .... Nebraska, Oklahoma, Utah
Superior .... Huron, Ontario, Michigan,
                  Erie
Newfoundland .. Manitoba, Ontario, Yukon
boundary .... border, line
• High-frequency words: where, one, another, usually,
by, into, their

Page 47—Princess Furball

cruel .... mean, hateful
chose .... decided
lonely .... unhappy, alone
princess .... girl, child, baby
beautiful .... pretty, gorgeous
promised .... gave, sold
furious .... angry, upset, frightened, poor
• High-frequency words: there, was, to, because, who,
know, beautiful, very, one

Pages 48-49—Amelia's Notebook

transferred ...... moved, relocated
notebook .... journal, pad
claimed .... accepted, took
types .... kinds, sorts
contents .... stuff, thoughts
private .... secret, personal
journal .... diary, log
travels .... journeys, adventures, feelings
pasted .... glued, stuck, taped, put
fascinating .... interesting, unique
peers .... friends, buddies, classmates
• High-frequency words: who, new, school, about,
what, was, with, anyone, journal, people, very, they,
too, write, to

Pages 50-51—Alexander Who Used to be Rich Last Sunday

relatives .... grandparents, uncles, friends
suggested .... recommended
wasted .... used, spent
vanished .... disappeared, gone
predictions .... guesses, statements
neighbor .... friend, buddy
disappearing .... vanishing, going
furious .... angry, upset, mad, sorry
shouting .... screaming, yelling, saying
penniless .... poor
• High-frequency words: two, something, with, about,
could, was, too, when, their, again, very

Pages 52-53—Sootface

daughter .... girl, child
cruel .... mean, hateful, ugly
chores .... work, jobs
frightened .... terrified, scared, sad, angry
village .... town, camp, country
power .... talent, ability
wife .... friend
prove .... show, demonstrate
beautiful .... lovely, pretty, good
dishonest .... lying, untruthful
locate .... find, seek
noticed .... found, saw
handsome .... tall, strong
correctly .... honestly, truthfully
• High-frequency words: two, beautiful, they, off, with,
were, when, could, wear, went, was, who, into, to,
where, because

Pages 54-55—Third Graders

somewhere .... somewhere
preferences ...... choices
grown-ups .... adults, parents
gymnastics .... skating, baseball
phone .... computer, Internet
chatterboxes ..... talkers
topics .... subjects things
collaborative .... cooperative, supportive
projects .... activities, reports
recorders .... writers, timers
favorite .... best, newest
siblings .... children, brothers, friends
• High-frequency words: are, school, they, enough,
also, about, their, have, with, when, by, favorite

Pages 56-57—Sleepovers and Campouts

convincing .... asking, begging
selecting .... picking, choosing
choosing .... selecting, renting
snacks .... treats, munchies, food
popcorn .... chips, candy
promises .... agreements, decisions
silence .... quiet, snoring
daylight .... morning, sunrise
conclusion .... decision, vote
• High-frequency words: have, to, want(ed), your,
their, by, are, through, off, everybody, almost,
because

Page 58—Writing a Paper

challenge .... task, job
selecting .... choosing, finding, picking
narrowing .... limiting, picking
taking .... receiving, accepting, getting,
                  making
circling .... underlining, marking
proofreading .... rereading, checking
replacing .... changing, trading
several .... many, some
• High-frequency words: it's, to, write, sometimes, with,
when, are

Page 59—Similes

strong .... powerful
flip .... turn, swim, dive
cheetah .... panther, lion
beautiful .... pretty, gorgeous
trembles .... shakes
clever .... smart, intelligent
smart .... intelligent, clever
clown .... comedian
• High-frequency words: when, to

Guess the covered word.

Page 60—Memories

treasures .... keepsakes, things
capture .... save, preserve, keep
preserved .... saved, kept
through .... with, in, by
draw .... create, imagine
- High-frequency words: don't, to, are, journal(s), write, through, there, again

Page 61—Memory Treasures

club .... group
tucked .... hidden, stuck
wrapped .... packaged, used
present .... there
childhood .... youth, club
journal .... book, diary, record
special .... sweet, unique
- High-frequency words: journal, their, to, its, one, with, they, when, was

Transparency A—Reasons for Rainbows

rainbows .... clouds
reasons .... explanation, reasons
travels .... roams, moves, goes
straight .... long, short
speed .... velocity
spectrum .... rainbow
separated .... divided, parted
special .... unique, nice, pretty, different
keeper .... caretaker, guardian, maker
- High-frequency words: about, where, they, know, through, into, thought, usually, its, with

Transparency B—Savings Through Advertisements

bargain .... sale, savings
vocabulary ...... words, terms
free .... complimentary, cheap
savings .... change, money
regularly .... always, forever, again
customers .... shoppers, people
discount .... savings, sale, free
popular .... enjoyed, liked, favorite(s)
- High-frequency words: everybody, usually, buy, one, your, have, are, to, through

Transparency C—Kwanzaa

celebration ...... holiday, festival
fruits .... harvest, food
festival .... holiday, event
highlighted ...... featured, honored
virtues .... traits, components
decorate .... clean
- High-frequency words: there, by, are, their

Transparencies D-E—Air Jordan

character .... personal, individual
sports .... special, basketball
youngster .... kid, boy, child
practiced .... dribbled, leaped, shot
recognized ...... seen, noticed, cheered
trademark ...... special, unique, incredible
worldwide .... everywhere
scoring .... winning, points
championship ... win, title
promotes .... sells, advertises
concern .... love, compassion
- High-frequency words: who, by, people, one, always, was, with, to, their, where, when

Transparencies F-G—Milo and the Magical Stones

small .... tiny, little, big, large
gathering .... collecting, finding, getting
freezing .... cold, frosty
glittering .... beautiful, pretty
glowing .... sparkling, shiny
contribute .... give, offer
possible .... different, likely
disastrous .... terrible, unhappy, sad
create .... imagine, plan, write
silver .... shiny, aluminum
- High-frequency words: with, when, their, off, they, were, something, two, one, to, want(ed), your

Transparency H—Lon Po Po: Chinese Red Riding-Hood

Chinese .... new, different, Asian
version .... story, tale
daughters .... girls, sisters, children
humongous ...... large, giant
discovers .... finds, sees
convince .... persuade, tell
bothers .... pesters, tricks, sees
- High-frequency words: their, to, again, where, they

Transparencies I-J—Reading Adventures

climbing .... jumping, hopping, riding
mind .... thinking, imagination
place .... location, setting, neighborhood
setting .... location, place, city
meet .... see, imagine
travel .... move, wander, go
transportation .. movement, changing, going
vacation .... trip, adventure
wonderful .... fantastic, great
choose .... select, decide
control .... charge
trails .... adventure, traveling
- High-frequency words: your, when, about, people, there, know, were, no, one, another, could, where, wear, through, with, want, are, your, who, to, by

Transparency K—Yummy Pizza

love .... enjoy, like, want
stuffed .... filled, topped
tasty .... delicious, yummy
pepperoni .... onions, peppers, sausage
leftovers .... crumbs
- High-frequency words: always, to, favorite, with, when, about, are, don't